WNBA
NEW YORK LIBERTY
Carla Mooney

Mitchell Lane
PUBLISHERS

mitchelllanepub.com

2001 SW 31st Avenue
Hallandale, FL 33009

First Edition, 2026.
Author: Carla Mooney
Designer: Ed Morgan
Editor: Tammy Gagne

Series: WNBA
Title: New York Liberty

Library bound ISBN: 979-8-89260-484-0
eBook ISBN: 979-8-89260-489-5

Photo credits: p. 5 Shutterstock; p. 21, 23 wikimedia; balance Alamy

CONTENTS

Chapter ONE
A SUPERTEAM FORMS

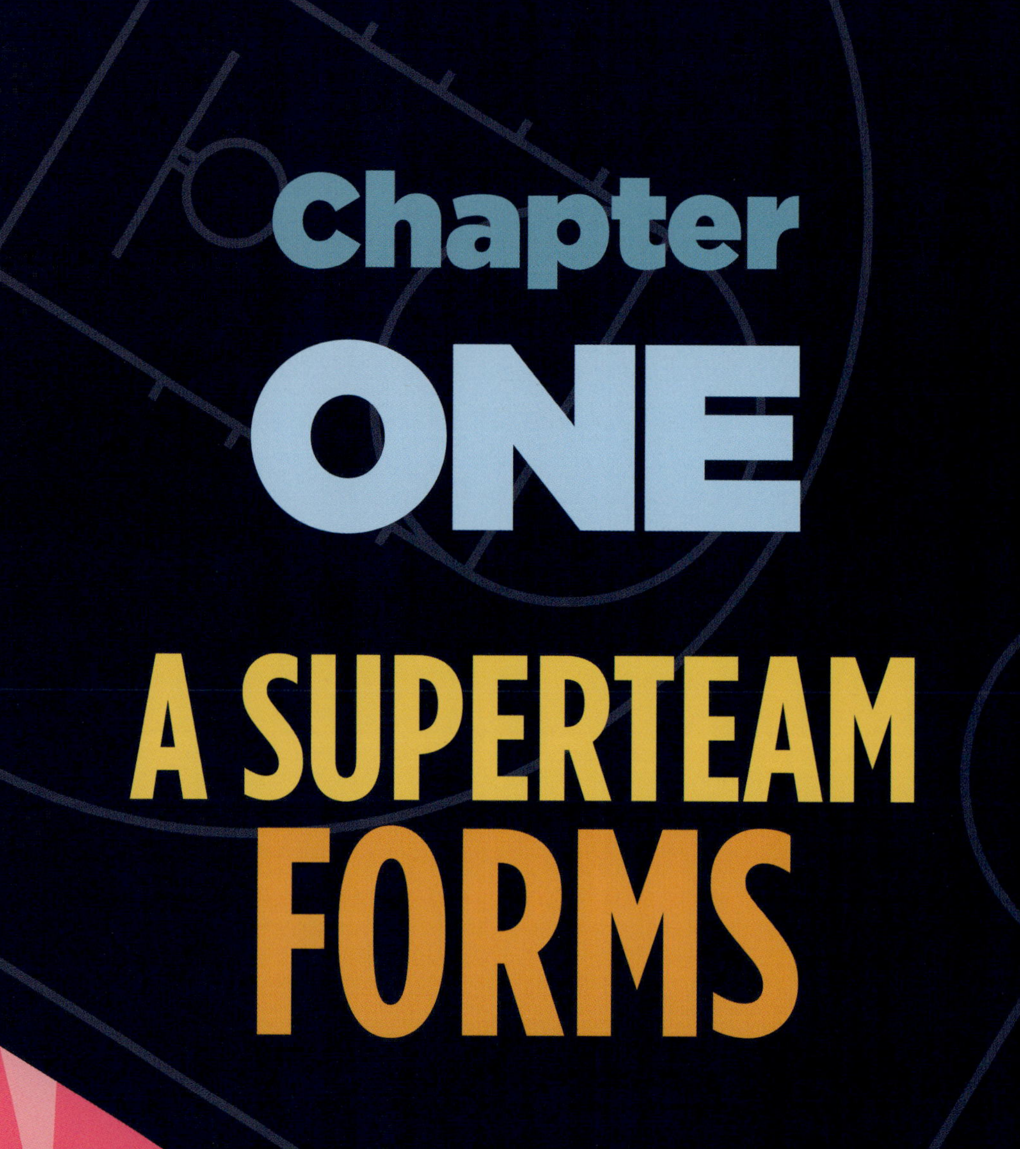

Breanna Stewart looks for the ball in a game for the Seattle Storm.

On February 1, 2023, Women's National Basketball Association (WNBA) superstar Breanna Stewart sent a tweet that shocked the sports world. Stewart posted a photo of New York's Empire State Building beside a TikTok video of her revealing a New York Liberty T-shirt. For six seasons, Stewart had been a top **forward** for the Seattle Storm. During that time, Stewart and the Storm won two WNBA championships, in 2018 and 2020. Now, Stewart was a **free agent**. She chose to sign with the New York Liberty.

CHAPTER ONE

Stewart talked about her decision in a 2023 interview. “I decided to go to New York because I want to continue to be great. And I want to go to the place where I can continue to help this league become better, to continue to raise the standard. And I feel like why not go to the biggest market in all of sports. And I’m really excited to go after their first championship,” she told ESPN.

The Stewart signing was not the Liberty’s only big move during the 2023 offseason. A month earlier, the Liberty traded for Jonquel Jones, the 2021 WNBA MVP from the Connecticut Sun. Jones was a 6-foot, 6-inch (2-m) forward/center and one of the WNBA’s top players. One day after Stewart’s announcement, another WNBA star joined the Liberty. **Point guard** Courtney Vandersloot announced she was also joining the Liberty. Vandersloot played twelve seasons with the Chicago Sky and won the WNBA title with that team in 2021.

A Superteam Forms

Jonquel Jones (right) takes a shot as Kamilla Cardoso defends for the Chicago Sky.

CHAPTER ONE

Excitement was growing in New York. Stewart, Jones, and Vandersloot were joining a team with young stars Sabrina Ionescu and Betnijah Laney-Hamilton. For the first time in years, the Liberty had championship talent. With so many good players, the Liberty was called a superteam. It had one goal in mind: winning the WNBA championship. It would be the Liberty's first championship title.

Liberty general manager Jonathan Kolb talked about the team's focus in an interview. "It's fantastic that we have this **roster** that's coming together, but we have a lot of work to do. Great, this looks awesome on paper, but let's make it work on the court," he told *Sports Illustrated*.

After continuing to dominate through the playoffs, the Liberty beat the Minnesota Lynx in game five of the finals, with a score of 67–62. New York finally earned its first championship in 2024.

A Superteam Forms

Breanna Stewart catches a pass from a teammate and prepares to shoot the basketball.

FAST FACT

Breanna Stewart enjoys juggling basketballs for fun.

Chapter TWO

SO CLOSE

The New York Liberty logo features a torch with a basketball-like flame.

The New York Liberty is one of the eight original teams in the WNBA. The Liberty was formed in 1997 and plays in New York City. The team's name comes from a well-known New York landmark, the Statue of Liberty.

CHAPTER TWO

In its first season, the Liberty established itself as a strong team. The Liberty went 17–11 in the regular season and made the playoffs. The team advanced to the first WNBA Finals but lost to the Houston Comets.

The Liberty remained a strong team in the 1990s and early 2000s. New York reached the WNBA Finals again in 1999, 2000, and 2002. But the team lost each time.

In 2003, the Liberty had its first losing season, missing the playoffs. The team entered a **rebuilding** phase. Some years, the team made the playoffs. Other years, it did not.

From 1997 to 2018, the Liberty played home games at Madison Square Garden. In 2015, Joe Tsai, the WNBA's Brooklyn Nets owner, bought the Liberty. The team moved its home games to the Barclays Center in Brooklyn in 2020.

So Close

Guard Kamiko Williams drives down the court with the basketball during a 2013 game.

CHAPTER TWO

In 2020, the Liberty **drafted** guard Sabrina Ionescu. She proved to be a great addition to Laney-Hamilton, Stewart, and Vandersloot. The new lineup had an immediate **impact**. The Liberty went 23–8 in the 2023 season. They advanced to the WNBA Finals for the fifth time.

The Liberty lost to the Las Vegas Aces in the championship series. Yet Liberty coach Sandy Brondello remained hopeful about the future. "Just to get to a final, it's not easy. This is our first year together. . . . Things obviously we know can still get better, but overall just really proud of the group," Brondello said in an interview with *Sports Illustrated*.

So Close

Liberty player Rebecca Allen looks for an opening while being guarded by two Seattle Storm players in 2021.

FAST FACT

The documentary *Unfinished Business* tells the story of the WNBA and follows the NY Liberty's 2021 season.

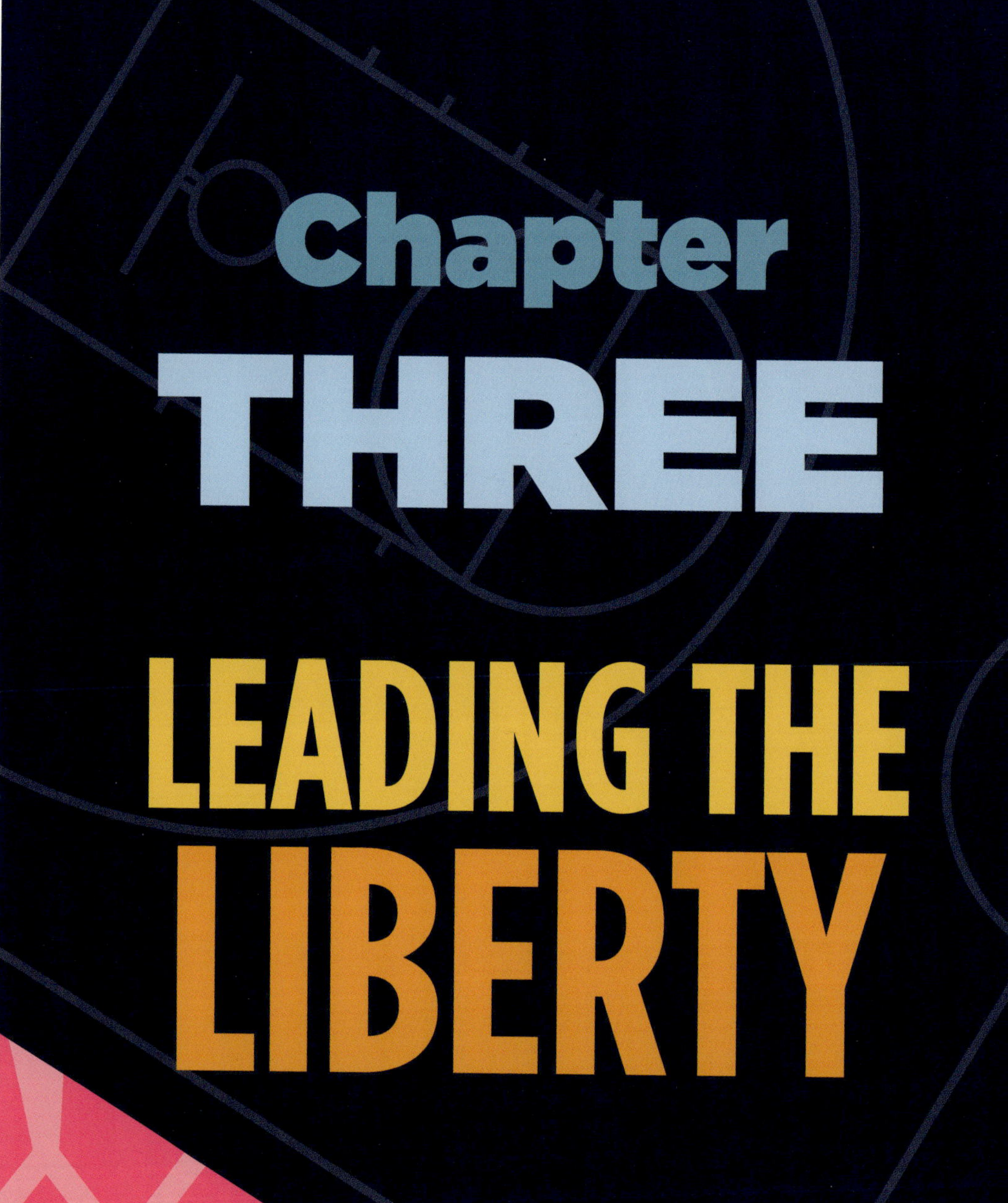

Chapter THREE

LEADING THE LIBERTY

Several coaches have led the Liberty. Nancy Darsch was the Liberty's first head coach. Darsch was a successful college coach at Tennessee State and Ohio State. In two seasons, Darsch set the Liberty on the path to early success.

CHAPTER THREE

Richie Adubato coached the Liberty from 1999 to 2003. He led the team to three WNBA Finals—in 1999, 2000, and 2022. When the Liberty struggled in the 2004 season, the team fired Adubato. A series of coaches followed. They included Anne Donovan, a gold-medal-winning Olympic coach, and Bill Laimbeer, a former National Basketball Association (NBA) player.

In 2022, the Liberty hired Sandy Brondello. She was a WNBA **veteran** and coach. Brondello spoke about the opportunities for women coaches in a 2022 interview. "It means a lot. We're all coaches. We're not female coaches, we're not male coaches, we're basketball coaches. Still, it's good to see women getting those opportunities. Former players getting those opportunities," she said in an article on *The Local W*.

Leading the Liberty

Veteran Liberty coach Sandy Brondello directs her players as she stands courtside.

CHAPTER THREE

Brondello quickly made an impact. In 2022, the Liberty went 16–20 and lost to the Chicago Sky in the first round of the playoffs. In 2023, the Liberty finished with a record of 32–8. The team advanced to the finals for the fifth time in team history. However, the Liberty lost to the Las Vegas Aces. They still did not have a title.

Brondello and the Liberty continued to push toward the WNBA Championship in 2024. Racking up many wins against the other Eastern Conference teams, they were hopeful as the league approached the postseason. It was looking like 2024 might be the New York Liberty's year.

Leading the Liberty

Joe Tsai and Clara Wu

FAST FACT

Clara Wu and Joe Tsai bought the Liberty in 2019. They are also co-owners of the Brooklyn Nets.

Chapter FOUR

TOP PLAYERS

Breanna Stewart is one of the Liberty's biggest stars. She entered the WNBA in 2016 with the Seattle Storm. Stewart quickly became one of the WNBA's best players. She won two championships and earned numerous individual awards. In 2018, Stewart was named the league's Most Valuable Player (MVP).

CHAPTER FOUR

In 2023, Stewart joined the Liberty. In her first season with the team, Stewart averaged 23 points, 9.3 **rebounds**, and 3.8 **assists** per game. She set a new career high for scoring and assists. She also set a league record with four 40-point games. Although the team fell short of a title, Stewart won the WNBA MVP award.

In 2020, the Liberty drafted guard Sabrina Ionescu first overall. However, Ionescu suffered a severe ankle sprain in her third game with the team. She missed the rest of the 2020 season.

Ionescu returned healthy for the 2021 season. In 2022, she became the first WNBA player with more than 500 points, 200 rebounds, and 200 assists in a single season. She also scored 1,000 career points in just 66 games, the most in such a short time for a player drafted by the Liberty. Ionescu was named a WNBA All-Star in 2022, 2023, and 2024.

Liberty players Sabrina Ionescu (left) and Brianna Stewart (right) pose with professional soccer player Lucy Bronze.

FAST FACT

Breanna Stewart and Sabrina Ionescu won gold medals with the U.S. women's national basketball team at the 2024 Paris Olympics.

CHAPTER FOUR

Jonquel Jones is the Liberty's towering center. The 2021 WNBA MVP joined the Liberty in 2023. Jones talked about her desire for a title in a 2023 interview. "I've done a lot of things in my career. One of the only things that I haven't done is walk away with a championship. I wanted to go to a place where I would have a good chance to do that and play with people I respect," she told *GQ Sports*.

The team led the league for most of the season and went on to win their first championship.

Top Players

The starting five for the Liberty are a fearsome dream team (left to right): Betnijah Laney-Hamilton, Courtney Vandersloot, Breanna Stewart, Jonquel Jones, and Sabrina Ionescu.

GLOSSARY

assists
Passes made to teammates, which lead to scored points

drafted
Selected to join a team

forward
A basketball player who plays near the basket, often rebounding and scoring goals

free agent
A player who is free to sign a contract with any team

impact
Having a strong effect on someone or something

point guard
A basketball player who brings the ball up the court and sets up offensive plays

rebounds
Caught basketballs after missed shots

rebuilding
Starting over to make a strong team

roster
A list of players on a sports team

veteran
A player with extensive experience

SLAM DUNK WNBA TRIVIA

- Ellie the Elephant is the New York Liberty's mascot. She wears a Statue of Liberty crown.
- Liberty fans are known as Liberty Loyalists.
- The team's colors are black, white, and seafoam green.
- Because of the high demand for tickets, the Liberty was the first WNBA team to have a waitlist for premium seats.
- The Timeless Torches, a dance group of men and women over age forty, perform at every Liberty home game.
- The Liberty has retired two jersey numbers, Teresa Witherspoon's number 11 and Becky Hammon's number 25.

FIND OUT MORE

IN PRINT

Chandler, Matt. *Sabrina Ionescu*. Capstone Press, 2022.

Davidson, B. Keith. *WNBA*. Crabtree Publishing, 2022.

Mooney, Carla. *Seattle Storm*. Mitchell Lane Publishers, 2026.

ON THE INTERNET

***New York Liberty*.**
https://liberty.wnba.com.

"New York Liberty," *ESPN*, n.d.
www.espn.com/wnba/team/_/name/ny/new-york-liberty.

"New York Liberty," *FOX Sports*, n.d.
www.foxsports.com/wnba/new-york-liberty-team.

INDEX

About the Author

Carla Mooney is the author of many books for young adults and children. She lives in Pittsburgh, Pennsylvania, with her husband and three children. She enjoys watching all types of sports, including women's basketball.